GUIDE TO
TROUBLED BIRDS

For Kim

Second Edition

www.mincingmockingbird.com

Printed in Canada

ISBN 978-0-615-35804-8

The Mincing Mockingbird

GUIDE TO
TROUBLED BIRDS

An authoritative illustrated compendium
to be consulted in the event of an infant or small child
being torn apart by a murder of crows

Revised and Enlarged Edition

He gave them the heebie-jeebies.

He had nothing else to give.

"I'll even kill your *soul*."

I WISH SOMEONE HAD TOLD YOU THE FATAL FOLLY OF GETTING ON THE BAD SIDE OF A GROSBEAK, BUT ALAS, YOUR FATE IS SEALED

"When God opens the book to search for your name, any mention of you will have been scratched out so furiously that the paper will be scored through four pages deep. The only proof that you even existed will be only through the memory of those who knew you, and I'll make certain that anyone who ever crossed paths with you, any stranger who said 'gesundheit' after you sneezed—I will ensure that all those loose ends will be tied in a knot of bloody finality."

Dude, I just shooed you away from my fries is all—

"IT BEGINS!"

"Who do I have to blow for some seed?"

IT IS ONLY AN EXPRESSION
FOR GOD'S SAKE, BUT,
I MEAN, SERIOUSLY,
HOW ABOUT IT,
I AM STARVING TO DEATH

"I fly 4,000 miles non-stop, to find the place blanketed in snow? Do you have any clue how many calories I've burned? Do you know how cold it is, flying against a headwind 200 feet in the air? I nearly die to get here and the freaking feeder is EMPTY? You have *got* to be kidding me.

I will tap this window with my beak until someone either fills up that feeder or answers my question."

Tap tap tap.

Tap tap tap.

Tap tap tap.

"Pull up!"

THE WIND CARRIED
AWAY MY WORDS,
RENDERING THEM USELESS

"I watched in horror as the Johnson's living room picture window loomed before his swooping form.

I screamed, 'It's a window, you dumb bastard!
A *window*!'

The sound came to me finally, delayed by distance.
It sounded like a wet sock slapping against concrete.

I loved him."

"I heart Tippi Hedren."

HITCHCOCK NOT THE ONLY ONE WITH A THING FOR BLONDES

"I liked working with her. She was real nice. She'd say 'hi' at the craft services table, wasn't a bitch, you know? A real classy lady.

I'm not afraid to admit I made a pass at her. Clumsy, mostly just squawking and some feather-ruffling...I don't regret doing it. That voice just drove me bonkers.

Hitch simply raised an eyebrow, but it was enough to put me in my place."

(Little-known Tippi Hedren fact: during the filming of *The Birds*, Ms. Hedren would have a crew member put a canvas sack full of live, angry finches over her head and cinch it at her neck with a velvet scarf. When she was needed for a shot, the sack was removed and the mangled carcasses removed. Ms. Hedren would say her lines, Hitchcock would say "cut," and only then would she spit out a woven, feathered bracelet. The last of the "Tippi bracelets" was sold at Christie's for $9,750.)

The ability to remain

sober and gracious

is, indeed,

a form of

mild insanity.

"Cats fear me."

OUNCE PER OUNCE, TOUGHER THAN A WOLVERINE

"I've taken an eye from a cat for every hummingbird brother and sister lost to their feline featherlust. And I'll take them until the burning furnace of rage that flares in my breast dies like the implosion of a sun. Until then, cat blindness will increase incrementally until every goddamned cat on the block is walking in circles."

"For reals?"

THIS IS A BIRD FEEDER, NOT A CHINESE BUFFET

I'm cutting you off. I'm done filling this feeder. From here on out it's only a yard decoration.

Aw, c'mon, man. Don't look at me like that. I see you out there every day—the flight from the tree branch to the lip of the feeder leaves you looking like you just ran up 12 flights of stairs. You're not looking so good. A bird's got to know when to say when. Just because the feeder is full up on seed does not mean that you have to eat it all in one sitting. For God's sake. Look at you. Have you even mated this year? Well, who would have you? Just because your heart beats 180 times a minute does not give you the right to eat like this. I can't even see your feet. You look like a feathered baseball. And I like a bird song as much as the next guy, but lately you've just been belching. The wife's complaining, dude. I gotta cut you off. You've just got an appetite that will never be satisfied, and I'm done enabling this part of it. I won't watch you eat yourself to death.

Okay, one more time. One more fill. Here you go. For old time's sake. You're such a pretty bird, you know that? You're one beautiful morbidly obese sonofabitch. That's it. Not so fast. You'll choke.

"God can't help you now."

HE MAY TRY, BUT WILL FAIL,
FOR I AM AN OWL

Owls are the most infamous killers in the bird world. Most of them are nocturnal with puffy heads and eyes like windows upon which are thrown shadows of nightmare. They like to confess to their killings, to the point of bragging. Owls distpatch their victims mostly through bludgeoning, and sometimes by strangulation. They're fond of a bit of scalping from time to time, though mostly for fun. A woman was killed by an owl for the crime of having clashing patterns on her outdoor furniture. A case from 1971 of owl-on-human necrophilia remains in dispute.

In stark contrast to the brutality of their crimes, owls are frequently described as educated and charming, though "smelly." In the darkness before dawn they can occasionally be seen running in gangs with escaped circus clowns and goth kids out past curfew. Their mating is an almost indescribable, difficult experience to observe, with the participants sometimes dying of pleasure. A Barn Owl (*Tyta alba*) once successfully impersonated a mailman for several months in St. Charles, Illinois. If you see an owl, or suspect someone may *be* an owl, play dead immediately, and play it like you're whoring for an Emmy. 134 species in the world; 18 in North America.

"I disembowel. It's what I *do*."

BIRD NOT PROUD OF IT, BUT IT DOES WHAT IT DOES—WHO AM I KIDDING, OF COURSE IT IS PROUD OF IT

"When I tell my prey I want them to open up to me, I usually mean with their feelings.

But sometimes it all goes red for a moment.

Eh, what are you going to do. It's instinct."

She was lovely and charming
almost a saint.
She told me she enjoyed
laughter and dancing
opera, jazz
and
getting very
very
very high

"This is wonderful!"

"This is going to be fine!"

"I love this!"

I was soon to change my mind, however.

"It's all fun until someone
gets eviscerated."

MOMMA DIDN'T SEW, SHE SHARPENED, SHARPENED UNTIL THAT STEEL SANG

I still remember my mother's warning as she handed out old lawn mower blades to the neighborhood kids, so we could play a spirited game of "Shin-hack Street Polo." My mom could sharpen a lawn mower blade like nobody's business, and when she would hand me mine, she'd whisper, "I gave it a few extra drags on the leather strop. Now go hack some shins for Momma."

Years later, I went to visit her at Pinecrest. She sat in a rocking chair, resplendent in her gleaming white straightjacket. Every so often I'd hold out a cigarette for her to gently drag on. Her eyes focused for a moment, as if she saw something out in the gloaming. She looked at me and smiled, as if seeing me for the first time.

I cleared my throat. "Do you remember the game, Momma? The game you invented for us kids?"

She looked at me, her eyes dancing. "I sure wish I could get out of this huggin' suit so I could fill my shoes full of applesauce," she said.

"I know, Momma." When I moved to pat her knee, she lunged. I barely avoided her teeth, the loud snap echoing across the wide lawn.

"You want some of this?"

SOMEHOW I THINK I AM TO RECEIVE IT NO MATTER WHAT I OFFER AS AN ANSWER

"So I'm at the park a few weeks back, right, and I chase a Frisbee over by this bush. This bird gets all up in my shit. I'm all 'I ain't botherin' you, man, I'm just playing Frisbee.' And he just fixes me with this gaze."

Ha ha. That's funny. A bird?

"Yeah, it's hilarious. See this? See how I ain't got a thumb or forefinger on my left hand? I'm dying of laughter."

Jeez.

"Yeah 'jeez.' My texting days are over. You understand me, dude? *I can no longer text.*"

It's okay. I—

"DID YOU HEAR ME? I CAN'T TEXT!"

Settle down...its okay...here, take my handkerchief. Compose yourself.

"I'm sorry. I'm sorry."

Don't be. You lost digits. And the ability to enter digits.

"I know...I just can't get that bird out of my mind, man. That freaking bird in the bush."

Did you get your Frisbee?

"Did I—did I get my *Frisbee*? NO, I did not get my FRISBEE. You know why? The bird was using it as a PLATE."

"You're a whore and that makes me sad."

PARROT GIVES AN HONEST ASSESSMENT, FROM HIS POINT OF VIEW

"Oh, so you've finally come home! And lookee here—you've brought a 'man-friend'! He certainly looks like your type. Dead in the eyes. Dim. I'm amazed he's got the mental capacity to keep his mouth from hanging open. Goodness, you're getting desperate. How many dates in are you going to get before you tell him about your white wine problem?

No—wait! Don't put the cover over the cage! No! Not the darkness! I'm sorry! I mean, you *are* a whore, but for what it's worth, I'm sorry! No! Not the endless dark!"

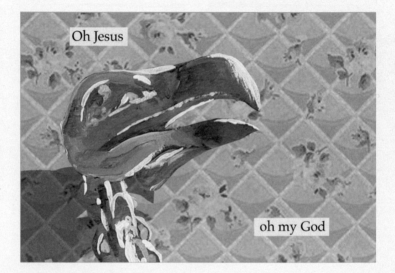

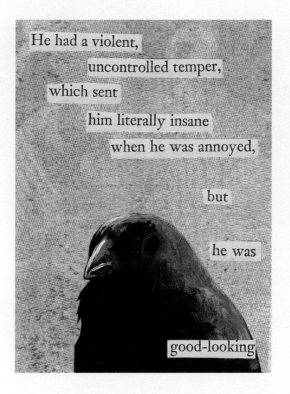

He had a violent,
uncontrolled temper,
which sent
him literally insane
when he was annoyed,

but

he was

good-looking

"Foie gras *this*, motherf---er!"

DUCK WOULD LIKE A WORD

"Sir?"

"Yes, what is it?"

"There is a duck here to see you."

"A what?"

"A *duck*, sir."

"Can't it wait? I'm eating."

"I'm afraid the bird will not be deterred. It is quite livid."

"All right. Can you cover this?"

"The foie gras, sir? Certainly."

"I'll only be a moment. Birds calling at all hours...they're worse than Jehovah's Witnesses."

"Sir, if I may mention...the bird has a pistol."

"A pistol?"

"I believe the 'kids' are calling them 'gats' these days, but yes, the bird is armed."

"Very damned odd all around. Well, I'll go have a word with the fellow, see if we can't get this straightened out. And fill my wine, won't you?"

"Of course, sir."

BLAMBLAMBLAMBLAMBLAMBLAMBLAMclickclick. Click.

"My mating dance is mostly seizures."

I CALL IT THE HIPPY HIPPY SHAKE, MY POTENTIAL MATES CALL IT DISTURBING AND OFF-PUTTING

We all can't be Fosse. Let me see a little of it.

Okay, okay that's enough—you're freaking me out. Stop it.

Stop.

"I can't."

"Two for flinching."

CHICKEN CANNOT ABIDE FLINCHERS

From the journal of Nebraska prairie farmer Eli Hardekopf, June 14, 1842:

Indians stormed the farm last night, but I done turned the chicken loose on 'em. Barnyard was still squishy from blood come mornin'. I do love that chicken. Mean cuss, though. But I do love him. I love that killin' fool with all my heart.

Note to self: go to town and place an ad for a mail-order bride. Remember to include "Must love chickens. If you have an ounce of chicken jealousy in your heart, stay home."

I can hear Indians out in the dark. The bird is near the door, scratchin' at the floor and making that low noise in his throat. He's got that gleam in his eyes. Better let him out.

Note to self: install chicken door.

"F--k your windshield!"

BIRD CHOOSES LAST WORDS TO BE THOSE OF DEFIANCE, AND THUS SHOWS MORE COURAGE THAN MOST

"Oh, dear, honey—look out for that bird—oh, no. You hit it. You killed it."

"It flew into our windshield. I'm not swerving to avoid some stupid bird," he said.

"It sounded like it actually...spoke. Like it said something."

"I've told you time and time again that you need to stop at your first glass of wine. Now please be quiet and let me drive."

She looked out into the fading light and felt tears on her cheeks, a strange fear coming over her. The only sound was the hum of the tires.

"Honey," she said.

"What?"

Her mouth opened and closed wordlessly until the sounds came. "I think it said, 'F--k your windshield.'"

He drove in silence for a long while, and she couldn't see his face in the dark.

Finally he said, "I think you're right," his voice small and hollow.

"I either have West Nile or syphilis."

BUT I NEVER SAW PARIS

"It's both? Man. I really had an irresponsible streak there. There was just too much youth in me, and the world lay before me like a lover. I just dove in. The week in Tijuana with Manuela the junkie lady who was really a man, was, in hindsight, a mistake.

But I *lived*.

This itching is driving me into madness. It really is. Saints preserve us, that itches. Whoo-boy. Can you itch that for me? No? I understand. No, it's okay. Still. Man. Woooow. That's some itchiness there. That is bad. Can you just get in there and—? No, no. Whew."

"I'd sell you to Satan for one corn chip."

BIRD LETS YOU KNOW YOUR VALUE IN A TRADE, AND HE IS BEING MIGHTY GENEROUS

———————◆———————

"For a bag of corn chips—not even a big bag, but one of those little bags that say 'Not for Resale,' or even fingernail-shaped 'corn snacks' from the dollar store—I'd tear down this whole far-reaching, malicious world.

Damn. I got a hankerin' for corn chips somthin' fierce.

Not those hot ones, though. I'm talking standard corn chips."

"Oh. You're an *artist*."

OWL IS NOT IMPRESSED

"Isn't that simply magnificent. Please excuse my yawn.

Don't let my presence give you pause. Fiddle with your paints and palette. Waste your days on whims and prancing through the daisy fields of inspiration.

You are boring me with your 'specialness' and your 'talent.'

Now bring me a juicy mouse or BEGONE!"

"It's the po-po!"

BIRD JUST NEEDS TO GET
OUT OF TOWN FOR A WHILE

"Officer, I was just riding with this bird down to the corner to get some cigarettes. No, I do not know this feathered gentleman. Yes, that is a crack pipe. Yes, sir, I did do that tattoo myself. I used a waffle iron, sir. I just colored in the burns with a Sharpie. Now, it's funny you ask, because I get asked if I have anything sharp in my pockets quite often, and I have to say it has become a monotonous dirge. No sir, I will not put my hands behind my back, in fact I'm pretty sure that I'm going to try and run, though I'm fairly certain I will be caught within half a block and then I expect you'll taser me until I'm crying and begging for you to kill me. Usually that's when you sic the dog on me. Well, I guess I'd better get this underway. Sometimes I think my life is just one bitter, endless circle of tragedy.

A bitter, endless circle of tragedy made tolerable by the crack cocaine mind orgasms."

"Don't get jealous on me."

BABY, NOT THIS AGAIN

"I'm telling you for the last time. I was at the bird bath, behind the Johnson's two-story on Maple. Minding my own business, maybe preening a bit. Gettin' a sheen on. She flew out of the sun. It was over so quick. It meant nothing. I never saw her again. She was a Western Tanager! What was I supposed to do—*ignore* her? Look, maybe if you had a uniformly olive head, back and rump with whitish wing linings and faint wing bars—wait, I'm sorry! Baby! I didn't mean it! Come back. Baby!"

"Unicorn of Love, impale me!"

LOVE IN THE TIME OF CRYSTAL METH

First of all, I told you to lay off the Devil's dandruff. Second, while you're on it, you should not be on Internet dating sites.

And third, Cupid is not a mystical horse with a brain horn.

"I'm a dirty bird."

SADOMASOCHIST WOODLAND CREATURE TELLS IT LIKE IT IS

"No birdbath is going to clean *me* up. I've been very, very bad, and I need to be tied up in a fine filament net and have a metal identification band put around my leg. Are you up for that?

Can you handle it?

I want you to clip my wings. I need to be punished.

The safe word is 'suet.'"

"I puke in my kids' mouths."

LET'S STICK WITH REGURGITATION

"Now listen, Mommy had kind of a rough night at the bar last night, so I'm not sure how much of this is small amounts of partially digested bits of protein-rich nuts and seeds and how much of it is onion rings and apple-flavored schnapps.

Oh, God, here it comes. I mean - dinner's ready!"

I preen for Satan.

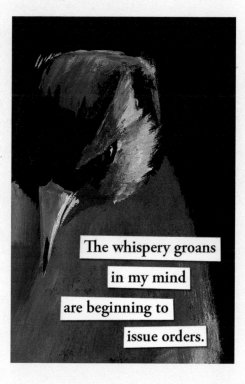

The whispery groans
in my mind
are beginning to
issue orders.

"You do *what* with my eggs?"

THE DOG FINALLY TALKED

"We worked on him in the henhouse for over an hour, but he finally gave it up. The waterboarding wasn't working, so we 'reassessed' our interrogation techniques. For what it's worth, we told him 'good dog' before he died.

But down to the matter at hand. This information is, as you can imagine, quite disturbing to us. Now, I want you to know the house is surrounded by fowl in every direction. You'd make it as far as the clothesline, and...well. Let's just say the dog was treated kindly in comparison to what would transpire on that brown and trampled ground.

The offer I make is this: give us back the uneaten eggs and we'll let the woman and the children live. We'll give you five minutes. Just say your fare-thee-wells and tell the woman we expect to continue to be fed and watered, and we will raise our young in peace. Refuse this offer, and all manner of beaked and flapping hell will come through glass and wood until by dawn the farm will be ours and you all but a memory, something that owned the land for a time but was given up to it.

Anyway, I'll be out here in the barnyard.

I'll just leave the dog collar here on the step."

BIRD ATTACK STATISTICS 1974

Table 1. Bird attacks: body parts injured	
Calf/knee	10
Thigh	14
Eyes	985
Arms	25
Feet	0
Hair extensions	5
Pancreas	4
Buttocks	99
Fingers	86
Abdomen/stomach	9
Head	54
Cankles	293
Back	8
Cellulite	210
Genitals	834

Table 2. Bird attacks: nature of wounds	
Severe lacerations	46
Significant loss of tissue	37
Bone exposed	12
Scalping	21
Good old-fashioned disemboweling	2
Waste burns	31
Raking	4
Cut by stinging remarks	5
Body skeletonized	52
Appendage lost to bird	17
Lobotomy through nostril	8
Feelings hurt	42
Swallowed whole or presumed so	16

(Body not recovered in 7 cases.)

STUDY QUESTIONS

1. How many species of warblers are known?

2. What species of bird makes its nest in the body cavity of a dead bird?

3. How much performance-enhancing dope should you give a four pound rooster before a cockfight? Do you think I gave it too much? Oh, jeez. I think I gave it too much. Why is it doing that? Oh, man.

4. *Why is it doing that?* That is not—ah, God. What should I do? *Make it stop doing that!*